TEN INDICTMENTS AGAINST THE
MODERN CHURCH

TEN INDICTMENTS AGAINST THE
MODERN CHURCH

Paul Washer

Reformation Heritage Books
Grand Rapids, Michigan

Ten Indictments against the Modern Church
© 2018 by Paul Washer

Reformation Heritage Books
2965 Leonard St. NE
Grand Rapids, MI 49525
616-977-0889 / Fax 616-285-3246
orders@heritagebooks.org
www.heritagebooks.org

Printed in the United States of America
18 19 20 21 22 23/10 9 8 7 6 5 4 3 2 1

Library of Congress Cataloging-in-Publication Data

Names: Washer, Paul, 1961- author.
Title: Ten indictments against the modern church / Paul Washer.
Description: Grand Rapids, Michigan : Reformation Heritage Books, 2018.
Identifiers: LCCN 2018027448 (print) | LCCN 2018029310 (ebook) | ISBN 9781601786289 (epub) | ISBN 9781601786272 (pbk. : alk. paper)
Subjects: LCSH: Church—Sermons. | Church—Biblical teaching—Sermons.
Classification: LCC BV603 (ebook) | LCC BV603 .W37 2018 (print) | DDC 262—dc23
LC record available at https://lccn.loc.gov/2018027448

For additional Reformed literature, request a free book list from Reformation Heritage Books at the above regular or e-mail address.

Contents

The Author's Prayer

Father, I come before You in the name of Your Son, Jesus Christ. Lord, You know all things. They are all before You like an open book. Who can hide their heart from Your presence and Your eye? The deeds of the most clever men are exposed before You. Your omniscience knows no bounds. And if it were not for grace, I would be of all men most terrified. But there is grace, abounding and glorious, poured out on the weakest of men, and abounding to Your glory. Father, I praise You and I worship You; I thank You for all that You are and all that You have done. There is no one like You in the heavens or the earth or under the earth. You are King and there is no other. You are Savior and You share that glory with no one.

Father, this day You know me and my great need of grace. Why am I here except that You called the weakest among men, the most ignoble among brothers, and that by Your grace the lesser oftentimes teaches the greater? That is always my case and I praise You. I worship You.

Father, help us today. To the wind with eloquence, and with the brilliant intellect, Father. Let the truth go forward. Let men be changed, that the state of Your church may be more glorious. I pray for grace upon grace and mercy upon mercy for myself and for those who hear. Help us, oh God, and we will be helped; and we will boast in that help. In Jesus's name we pray, amen.

Introduction

Now the Spirit speaketh expressly, that in the latter times some shall depart from the faith, giving heed to seducing spirits, and doctrines of devils.

—1 Timothy 4:1

It is a great privilege for a man to stand and speak, or write, about things such as revival, reformation, and the working of God among His people and among men. In this short book I am going to share with you an indictment. It is an indictment of hope.[1]

As I have prayed through what I should communicate to you, I have come to a great conclusion. A great

---

1. The material in this book was originally preached as a single sermon on a specific occasion. That sermon has been signally blessed by the Holy Spirit in the lives of many around the world, resulting in genuine conversions and the return of backsliders to God. This volume is not simply a transcript of that sermon. Most of the changes involve an attempt to turn spoken, more sermonic language into written, more literary language. All revisions have been carried out with the primary aim of honoring the meaning of the preacher, the spiritual intent in the sermon, and, above all, the God whose Word is being proclaimed.

burden is laid on my heart: *we need revival.* We need an awakening, but we cannot simply expect the Holy Spirit to come down and clean up all the mess we have made. We have clear direction from the Word of God with regard to what He has done through Christ. We know how He expects us to live. We know how He expects us to order His church. It does little good for men to cry out for extrabiblical manifestations of God's Spirit when clear biblical principle is violated all around us.

I want you to know that there is little need for the devil and evil men to oppose a man praying for revival unless that man is also laboring for reformation. We have been given truth. We cannot simply do what is right in our own eyes and then expect the Holy Spirit to come down and bless our labors.

As we look into the Old Testament, we see that Moses is given very detailed instructions on how to build the tabernacle (Ex. 25–28). Was that instruction given for Moses's sake or for the sake of the church? This passage is explaining that God is specific in His will. We are not to presume that we can take the smallest detail of God's revealed will and ignore it.

I know that I am a frail man. I am buffeted by many weaknesses. Nevertheless, I have an indictment. I cannot call it my indictment, because who am I to indict anyone? I dare not call it God's indictment, for how can I presume on His name? But I will say this: as I look around at the church and compare her to Scripture, I am persuaded that there are certain things that must change.

I do not claim to be another Martin Luther, whose writings and preaching inspired the Protestant Reformation and changed the course of Western civilization.[2] What follows is not intended as another ninety-five declarations nailed to a door in Wittenberg.[3] It is a burden on my heart that I must share.

Let me offer a warning. What I am going to say will anger some who read. It may be that you will accuse me of arrogance. It may be that you do not like my delivery. I have many times been arrogant, and I have many times delivered truth in a wrong way. Please do not allow my sins and errors to be an excuse for you. The question you must answer is this: Is what I am saying true, whether or not it is delivered through a faulty messenger?

Others will rejoice in what you hear, and you will want to say amen. But please do not indulge in crass triumphalism, because all of us bear a measure of guilt. If you have attained any degree of spiritual maturity, then I would say what my brother has said: "What hast thou that thou didst not receive? now if thou didst receive it, why dost thou glory, as if thou hadst not received it?" (1 Cor. 4:7). Would it not be better to worship God in humility?

If you are a younger minister, I do not want you to get caught up in these truths and take them back to storm your church without love. See to it that your knees are

---

2. Martin Luther (1483–1546) was a German theologian, university professor, and church reformer.

3. Luther posted ninety-five objections to the doctrine and practices of the Roman Catholic Church onto the door of the Castle Church at Wittenberg, Germany, on October 31, 1517. This was one of the major events that grew into the Protestant Reformation.

bleeding before you begin any sort of reformation! If you are an older minister serving the Lord for many years, I beg you not to be arrogant. An old foolish king can learn from the weakest of his servants.

I also beg this of you: have the courage to change everything, even if it is the last day of your life. At least you can go into glory knowing that you attempted a reformation that was biblical.

In addition, I will offer a warning to the older men. Please receive me carefully. I know the admonition in 1 Timothy 5:1, that I should not rebuke an older man but rather exhort him as a father. I do want to address you in that way. There is a great awakening going on in this country! It is happening not only in this country but also in Europe, South America, and many other places. I see young men going back to the rock from which we were cut. They are reading Charles Spurgeon[4] and George Whitefield.[5] They are still listening to Leonard Ravenhill,[6]

---

4. Charles H. Spurgeon (1834–1892) was an influential English Baptist minister who preached weekly to six thousand souls at the Metropolitan Tabernacle in London. His collected sermons fill sixty-three volumes.

5. George Whitefield (1714–1770) was the best-known evangelist of the eighteenth century and an itinerant preacher whom God greatly used in England and the American colonies during the Great Awakening.

6. Leonard Ravenhill (1907–1994) was an English Christian preacher and author who focused on the subjects of prayer and revival. He challenged the modern church to imitate the example of the first-century church in the book of Acts.

D. Martyn Lloyd-Jones,[7] A. W. Tozer,[8] and John Wesley.[9] It is a great movement, almost incredible! Just because the popular media or modern magazines such as *Christianity Today* have not discovered what is going on does not mean it is not happening! I want you to know that I never would have dreamed fifteen years ago that I would see the awakening I am seeing—not through my ministry but through what God is doing without any of our ministries.

I have seen in the Netherlands a thousand young men declaring, "Things have to change," crying out all night in prayer for the power of God and the truth of Scripture. I have seen people in South America recognizing that they have been so influenced by psychology and all sorts of superficial techniques coming from America with regard to evangelism. Now, weeping and broken, they are going back and truly evangelizing their churches. I have been in an inner city of the United States, sitting up at times until two and three in the morning discussing theology with young African Americans whom God is going to raise up to do more preaching than anyone will ever be able to imagine. There is an awakening!

---

7. David Martyn Lloyd-Jones (1899–1981) was a well-known Welsh preacher. After successful medical studies, he was pursuing life as a physician when God called him to preach the gospel. He is known for Christ-centered expository preaching.

8. Aiden Wilson Tozer (1897–1963) was an American Christian and Missionary Alliance pastor, preacher, and author. Known for deep personal piety and prayer, he often challenged the modern church to repent of shallowness and of compromise with the world.

9. John Wesley (1703–1791) was an Anglican minister and theologian. He is largely credited, with his brother Charles, with founding the English Methodist movement, which began when he took to open-air preaching in a similar manner to George Whitefield.

I say with tenderness that most people over forty do not have a clue about this awakening. Many young people are turning back to the great teachers from prior centuries. They are returning to the old ways, to truths that have brought awakening time and time again in this world. Most of these young men are just that—young! They will go to their leaders and say, "Look at what we have discovered! Look what happened in Wales.[10] Look what happened in Africa.[11] Look at this! Look at that! Look at this teaching! It is absolutely amazing!" And most of the older men today will either turn away or say, "It is nothing any different than what I have been preaching for twenty-five years." But it may be very different to what they have been preaching the last twenty-five years! And so we need to be very careful to understand that God is doing a work. Remember that "he which hath begun a good work in you will perform it" (Phil. 1:6).

Many people have the idea that they are going to "pray in" a revival. Other people say, "Revival will come whether you pray or not." I am not in either one of those camps. But I know one thing. When I see men, women, and young people all over the world praying for an awakening, to me that is the firstfruits of revival. And I can

---

10. Such as the Great Welsh Revival of 1904–1905, which began under the leadership of Evan Roberts (1878–1951), a twenty-six-year-old former coal miner and minister-in-training. The revival lasted less than a year, but in that period one hundred thousand converts were made and many churches returned to biblical faith.

11. I refer to the evangelization of sub-Saharan Africa beginning in the colonial period of the 1800s that continues today through both foreign missions and indigenous churches.

count on the fact that He who gives these firstfruits will bring in the full harvest.

In light of such matters, I want to look at ten indictments. I will set before you things I believe that we must change in the modern church.

1

A Practical Denial of the Sufficiency of Scripture

And that from a child thou hast known the holy scriptures, which are able to make thee wise unto salvation through faith which is in Christ Jesus. All scripture is given by inspiration of God, and is profitable for doctrine, for reproof, for correction, for instruction in righteousness: that the man of God may be perfect, thoroughly furnished unto all good works.

—2 Timothy 3:15–17

Over the last several decades, a mighty battle has been waged regarding the inspiration of Scripture. Some of you have not been a part of that battle, but many in more liberal denominations most certainly have. We have been in a battle for the Bible.

But there is a problem. When you come to believe as a people that the Bible is inspired, you have fought only half the battle. That is because the question is not merely "Is the Bible inspired—is it the inerrant Word of God?" The major question actually follows that: "Is the Bible sufficient, or do we have to bring in every so-called social science and cultural study in order to know how to run a church?" That is the great question! Social sciences, in my opinion, have taken precedence over the Word of God in such a way that most of us cannot even see it. It has so crept into our church, our evangelism, and our missiology that you barely can call what we are doing "Christian" anymore. Psychology, anthropology, and sociology have become primary influences in the churches.

Many years ago when I was in seminary, I remember a professor who walked in and started drawing footprints on the blackboard. And as he marched them across the blackboard, he turned to all of us and said only this: "Aristotle is walking through the halls of this institution. Beware, for I hear his footsteps more clearly than those of the apostle Paul, the team of inspired men who were with him, and even the Lord Jesus Christ Himself."

We have come to believe that a man of God can deal in certain tiny, restricted areas in the life of the church. However, when it really gets tough, we need to go to the social experts. That is an absolute lie! The Scriptures declare that they are given "that the man of God may be perfect, thoroughly furnished unto all good works" (2 Tim. 3:17). By means of the Bible we are adequately equipped for everything required of us.

What does Jerusalem have to do with Rome? And what do we have to do with those modern-day social sciences that were actually created as a protest against the Word of God? Why is it that evangelism, missions, and so-called church growth are shaped more by the anthropologist, the sociologist, and the Wall Street student who are up to speed on every cultural trend than by the Scriptures themselves? All the activity in our churches must be based on the Word of God. All the activity in missions must be based on the Word of God.

Our missionary activity, our church activity, and everything we do ought to flow from the theologian and the exegete—the man who opens up his Bible and has only one question: "What is Thy will, O God?" We are not to send out questionnaires to carnal people to discover what kind of church they would like to attend! A church ought to be friendly to genuine seekers, but the church ought to recognize that there is only one Seeker. His name is God! If you want to be friendly to someone, if you want to accommodate someone, accommodate Him and His glory, even if it is rejected by everyone else. We are not called to build empires. We are not called to be accepted by men. We are called to glorify God. And if you want the church to be something other than a distinctive people, a people marked out by holiness as belonging to the God of heaven (Titus 2:14; 1 Peter 2:9), then you want something that God does not want.

Listen to what Isaiah says: "They shall say unto you, Seek unto them that have familiar spirits, and unto wizards that peep, and that mutter" (Isa. 8:19). This could well be a description of the social scientists and the church growth gurus. Every two or three years all their major theories change. They have a new idea about what a man is and how you fix him, about what a church is and how you make it grow. Every two or three years there is another fad coming down the line about what can make your church into something super in the eyes of the world. Not so long ago one of the most well-known church growth experts said that he discovered he was entirely wrong on all his theories. But instead of turning people to Scripture—on his knees, broken and weeping—he embraced another man-made theory!

Such teachers give no clear word! Isaiah asks, "Should not a people seek unto their God? for the living to the dead? To the law and to the testimony: if they speak not according to this word, it is because there is no light in them" (Isa. 8:19–20). Should we as true churchmen—as preachers, as pastors, as Christians—go out and consult the spiritually dead on behalf of those whom the Holy Spirit has made alive? Absolutely not!

2

An Ignorance of God

*And the times of this ignorance God winked at; but
now commandeth all men every where to repent.*
                                                —Acts 17:30

At times I am asked to visit a place to preach a series on
the attributes of God. I often respond, "Well, brother, have
you thought this through?"

Someone might answer, "What do you mean, 'Have I
thought this through'?"

"Well, it is quite controversial, the subject that you are
giving me to teach in your church."

"What do you mean, it is controversial? It is God! We
are Christians. This is a church. What do you mean it is
controversial?"

I say, "Dear pastor, listen to me. When I begin instruct-
ing your people on the justice of God, the sovereignty of
God, the wrath of God, the supremacy of God, and the
glory of God, you are going to have some of your finest
and oldest church members stand up and say something
like this: 'That is not *my* god. I could never love a God like

that.' Why? Because they have a god they have made with their own mind, and they love what they have made."

Hear the Word of God:

> Thus saith the LORD, Let not the wise man glory in his wisdom, neither let the mighty man glory in his might, let not the rich man glory in his riches: but let him that glorieth glory in this, that he understandeth and knoweth me, that I am the LORD which exercise loving-kindness, judgment, and righteousness, in the earth: for in these things I delight, saith the LORD. (Jer. 9:23–24)

> These things hast thou done, and I kept silence; thou thoughtest that I was altogether such an one as thyself: but I will reprove thee, and set them in order before thine eyes. Now consider this, ye that forget God, lest I tear you in pieces, and there be none to deliver. (Ps. 50:21–22)

What is the problem? There is a lack of the knowledge of God. Many people hear this and think, "Oh, talking about the attributes of God and theology—that is all ivory tower stuff and has no practical application."

Listen to yourself speak! Do you really believe that the knowledge of God has no practical application? Do you know why all your Christian bookstores are filled with self-help books? It is because people do not know the true God! As a result they must be given all sorts of trivial devices of the flesh to keep them walking as sheep ought to walk! "Awake to righteousness, and sin not; for some have not the knowledge of God: I speak this to your shame" (1 Cor. 15:34). Why is there rampant sinning even among God's people? It is because of a lack of the knowledge of God!

When was the last time you attended a conference on the attributes of God? When was the last time, as a pastor, you taught for months on who God is? How much teaching in churches today has anything to do with who God is? It is so easy to go with the flow, to simply follow everybody else! But then one day you hear something like this and, all of a sudden, you realize that you can't even remember the last time you heard anybody teach on the attributes of God. No wonder we are the people that we are!

To know Him—that is what everything is about! To know Him is eternal life! Eternal life does not begin when you pass through the gates of glory. Eternal life begins with conversion. Eternal life is to know God. Do you honestly think you are going to be thrilled about walking down streets of gold for an eternity? The reason why you will not lose your mind in eternity is because there is One there who is infinite in glory, and you will spend an eternity of eternities pursuing Him, and finding Him, but you will never get your arms around even the foothill of His mountain!

Start now! There are so many different things you want to know and do, and so many books you want to read. Get a good book on God; get out your Bible and study it to know *Him*, to truly know the true and living God!

Because of all this, I would submit to you that in one sense it might be better in some so-called churches not even to have a Sunday morning service. Sunday morning is often the greatest hour of idolatry in the entire week because people are not worshiping the one true God. The great mass of people are worshiping a god formed out of their own hearts by their own flesh, by satanic devices, and by worldly intelligence. They have made a god just like themselves—a god who looks more like Santa Claus than He does Jehovah. There can be no fear of the Lord among us when there is no knowledge of the Lord among us.

3

A Failure to Address Man's Malady

As it is written, There is none righteous, no, not one: there is none that understandeth, there is none that seeketh after God. They are all gone out of the way, they are together become unprofitable; there is none that doeth good, no, not one.

—Romans 3:10–12

The book of Romans is one of my favorite books of the Bible. It is not a systematic theology. However, if you could say that any book in the Bible was a systematic theology, the letter to the church at Rome would be the closest. It is amazing that in this book Paul spends the first three chapters seeking to do one thing: to bring all men into condemnation. But condemnation is not the great *summum bonum*—the greatest and highest good—in his theology. Condemnation is not his final purpose. This pursuit of conviction of sin is a means to bring salvation to his readers because men must be brought to a knowledge of self before they will surrender themselves to God. You must cut away absolutely every hope in the flesh from fallen men before they will be brought to God.

That is important in everything, but it is especially important in evangelism. When I was twenty-one years old, and had just been called to preach, I walked into an old store in Paducah, Kentucky, where they sold suits to ministers for half price. They had been doing it for fifty or sixty years. All of a sudden, the door opened. I heard the bell ring as it closed. Standing there was an old man. I never caught his name, but he walked in and looked right at me. He said, "Boy, you have been called to preach, haven't you?"

I said, "Yes, sir."

The man was an old evangelist. He said, "You see where that building is right outside this building?"

I said, "Yes."

He said, "I used to preach there. The Spirit of God would come down and souls would be saved."

I said, "Sir, please tell me about it."

He said, "There wasn't anything like this evangelism today. We would preach for two and three weeks and give no altar call to sinful men. We would plow and plow the hearts of men until the Spirit of God began to work, and break their hearts."

I said, "Sir, how did you know when the Spirit of God was coming to break their hearts?"

He said, "Well, let me just give you one example. Many decades ago, I walked into this store to buy a suit. Someone had handed me $30 and said, 'Preacher, go buy yourself a suit tomorrow.' And when I walked through the door the young clerk taking care of the shop turned around and cried out, 'Who can save a wicked man like me?' And I knew that the Spirit of God had fallen on the place."

Today so many preachers just walk into a church building and talk to people, give them three exploratory questions, and ask them if they want to pray a prayer and ask Jesus to come into their heart. We make a twofold son of hell who will never again be open to the gospel because of the religious lie that we, as professing evangelicals, have spewed out of our mouth.

When we treat sin superficially, we are fighting against the Holy Spirit. It is said of Him that "when he is come, he will reprove the world of sin" (John 16:8). There are very popular preachers today who are more concerned about giving you "your best life now" than they are concerned about your eternal destiny. They are oblivious to the fact that they do not mention sin in their preaching. I can tell you that the Holy Spirit has nothing to do with their ministry, except to be working against it. Why? Because though a man may say that he has no ministry dealing with the sin of men, the Holy Spirit certainly does! It is a primary ministry of the Holy Spirit to come and convict the world of sin. When you do not deal specifically, passionately, and lovingly with men in their depraved condition, the Holy Spirit is nowhere around you.

We are deceivers when we deal with the malady of men lightly, like the shepherds of Jeremiah's day who "have healed also the hurt of the daughter of my people slightly, saying, Peace, peace; when there is no peace" (Jer. 6:14).

We are not only deceivers in doing this; we are immoral. We are like a doctor who denies his Hippocratic oath because he does not want to tell someone bad news. Perhaps he thinks that person will be angry with him or be sad. And so he does not tell his patient the news most necessary to save his or her life.

I hear preachers today, saying, "No, no! You don't understand! We are not like the culture that George White-field or Jonathan Edwards addressed.[1] We are not as hearty and vigorous as they were—we are broken. We don't have as much self-esteem—we are feeble, and we cannot take such preaching." Have you ever studied the lives of these men? Their culture could not bear what they preached either! No one has ever been able to bear the preaching of the gospel. Hearers will either turn against it with fierce-ness or be converted. And to say that we don't have as much self-esteem! Our world is overrun with this disgust-ing malady of self-esteem. Our greatest problem is that we esteem self more than we esteem God!

We are also thieves when we do not speak much about sin. This morning, where did all the stars go? Did some cosmic giant come by, pick them all up, throw them into a basket, and carry them someplace else? They were there, but you could not see them. But then the sky grows darker and darker, and as the night turns black as pitch, the stars come out in the fullness of their glory. When you refuse to teach the radical depravity of men, it is impos-sible to bring glory to God, His Christ, and His cross. The cross of Jesus Christ and its glory is most magnified when it is placed in front of the backdrop of our depravity. Luke speaks of a woman who loved much because she has been

---

1. Jonathan Edwards (1703–1758) was an American Congrega-tional preacher and evangelical theologian. He was well known for his preaching in the Great Awakening, along with George Whitefield.

forgiven much (Luke 7:47). She knew how much she had been forgiven because she knew how wicked she was.

But we are afraid to tell men of their wickedness, and they can never love God because of that. We have robbed them of the opportunity to boast not in self but to follow the admonition "he that glorieth, let him glory in the Lord" (2 Cor. 10:17).

4

An Ignorance of the Gospel of Jesus Christ

But God commendeth his love toward us, in that, while we were yet sinners, Christ died for us. Much more then, being now justified by his blood, we shall be saved from wrath through him.

—Romans 5:8–9

I submit to you that America and other Western countries are not gospel hardened. They are actually gospel ignorant, because so are most of their preachers. Let me repeat this. The malady in our countries is not liberal politicians, the root of socialism, Hollywood, or anything else. It is the so-called evangelical pastor, preacher, or evangelist of our day. That is where the malady is to be found. We do not know the gospel. We have taken the glorious gospel of our blessed God and reduced it to four spiritual laws, to five things God wants you to know, with a little nominal prayer at the end. And if someone repeats it after us with enough apparent sincerity, we popishly declare them to be born again! We have traded regeneration—the biblical doctrine of the new birth—for mere decisionism.[1]

---

1. Decisionism is the belief that "making a decision," usually

After I have preached about this, I am amazed at how many godly believers of thirty and forty years walking in the faith come up to me with tears, saying, "I never heard this before in my life." And yet it is the historical doctrine of redemption and propitiation.[2]

Let us define the issue very clearly. The gospel begins with the nature of God. It goes from there to the nature of man and his fallenness. These two great columns of the gospel set up for us what should be known in every believer's heart as "the great dilemma." What is that dilemma? It is the greatest problem in all of Scripture: if God is just, He cannot forgive you for your sin. How can God be just and at the same time the justifier of wicked men, when Scripture throughout the Bible says, as in the book of Proverbs, "He that justifieth the wicked, and he that condemneth the just, even they both are abomination to the LORD" (17:15)? And yet most of our historic Christian songs boast about how God justifies the wicked!

This is the greatest problem. This is the acropolis[3]— the great and high point—of the Christian's faith. So said Martyn Lloyd-Jones, Charles Spurgeon, and anyone else who has read and properly grasped the third chapter of the letter to the Romans. Preachers have got to set

---

practiced by walking a church aisle as a method of showing belief and/or praying a sinner's prayer, is equivalent to repenting of one's sins and trusting Christ alone for the pardon of that sin.

2. Redemption is the deliverance of God's elect from a state of sin into a state of salvation by the means and merit of the ransom paid by Christ on their behalf. Propitiation refers to appeasement—a sin offering that turns away the wrath of God.

3. This means "highest city" in Greek and was the fortified part of an ancient Greek city, usually built on a hill.

this before people. The great problem is that God is truly just and all men are truly wicked. God, to be just, must condemn wicked man. But then God, for His own glory, because of the great love with which He loved us, sent forth His Son, Jesus Christ, who walked on this earth as a perfect man. Furthermore, according to the eternal plan of God, the Lord Jesus went to the tree on Calvary. And on that tree, He bore our sin. Standing in the place of His people, bearing our guilt, He became a curse. "Cursed is every one that continueth not in all things which are written in the book of the law to do them" (Gal. 3:10). Christ redeemed us from the curse, becoming a curse in our place (Gal. 3:13).

So many people have a romantic, powerless view of the gospel. They see Christ hanging on the tree, suffering under the wounds of the Roman Empire. They imagine that the Father did not have the moral fortitude to bear the suffering of His Son, so He turned away. Not at all! The Father turned away because His Son became sin though He knew no sin!

And so, when Christ is in the garden and cries out, "Let this cup pass from me" (Matt. 26:39), people speculate, "Well, what was in the cup? Oh, it is the Roman cross. It is the whip. It is the nails. It is all that suffering." I do not want to take away from the physical sufferings of Christ on that tree, but the cup was the cup of God the Father's wrath that had to be poured out on the Son. Someone had to die, bearing the guilt of God's people, forsaken of God because of His justice, and crushed under the wrath of God—for it pleased the Lord to bruise Him (Isa. 53:10).

I was once in a Germanic seminary in Europe where I saw a book called *The Cross of Christ*.[4] I pulled it down and began to read. This is what it said: "The Father looked down from heaven at the suffering inflicted upon His Son by the hands of men, and counted that as payment for our sin." That is heresy! That physical suffering, that nailing to the tree—that was all part of the wrath of God. It had to be a bloody sacrifice; I will take nothing away from that. But if you stop there, you don't have the gospel.

When the gospel is preached today and shared in personal evangelism, do you ever hear of God's justice and wrath? Almost never! It is not made clear that Christ was able to redeem sinners because He was crushed under the justice of God. Having satisfied divine justice by means of the death of His beloved Son, God is now just and the justifier of the wicked.

Anything other than this is gospel reductionism! We wonder why it has no power. What has happened? I can tell you! When you leave the gospel behind and there is no longer any power in your supposed gospel message, then you have to do all the little tricks of the trade that are so prominently used today to convert men—and we all know most of them. But none of them work!

Several years ago, when graduating from seminary, God, in order to save my spiritual life, sent me to the middle of the jungles in Peru! And there I began to realize something. As Spurgeon said, "Greater men with greater minds than I have approached this doctrine of the Second Coming, but to no avail. It is a great and mighty

---

4. Not the well-known volume by John Stott.

doctrine." Therefore, he concluded, "I will set myself to this: seeking to comprehend something of Jesus Christ and Him crucified."

It makes me so angry when men treat the glorious gospel of Christ as though it were the first step into Christianity that takes only about ten minutes of counseling, and after that you go on to greater stuff. That shows you how pathetic we are in our knowledge of the things of God.

My friend, on the day of the second coming you will understand absolutely everything about the second coming, but through the eternity of heaven, you will scarcely begin to comprehend the glory of God at Calvary. It is what everything is about. Young man, young preacher, please take heed. Get at the truth of that tree. Grasp what it means! You will have no need or desire to offer strange fire in your censer (Lev. 10:1–3), if only you catch a glimpse of what Christ did on that tree.

I love to say this, and I have said it many times: Abraham takes Isaac up that mountain—his son, his only son whom he loved. Do you suppose the Holy Spirit was trying to tell us about something future? That son put up no struggle but laid himself down. And when that father surrendered his will to the will of God, he brought down that flint knife to pierce his own son's heart. But his hand was stayed, and the old man was told that God had provided a ram. So many Christians think, "Oh, what a beautiful end to that story." It is not the end; it is the intermission. Thousands of years later God the Father laid His hand on the brow of His Son, His only Son whom He loved, and took the flint knife out of the hand of Abraham and slaughtered His only begotten Son under the full force of His wrath.

Now do you know why that little gospel you preach has no power? Because it is no gospel! Get to the gospel. Spend your life on your knees. Get away from the teachings of unscriptural men. Study the cross!

The things we have just been saying actually grow out of ignorance of the doctrine of regeneration. I know that there are both Calvinists and Arminians, and I know that there are all sorts of strange views in between.[5] I call myself a "five point Spurgeonist"! But I want you to know this: Calvinism is not the issue. The issue is regeneration! And that is why I can have fellowship with Wesley, Ravenhill, Tozer, and others similar to them—because regardless of their errors on other issues, they believed that salvation could not be manipulated by the preacher but that it is a magnificent work of the power of almighty God. And, therefore, I stand with them on the necessity of a divine work of regeneration.

There is a greater manifestation of the power of God in the regenerating work of the Holy Spirit than in the creation of the world, of the whole universe, because He

---

5. Calvinists are those who believe, along with the French-born Swiss Reformer John Calvin (1509–1564), that the Bible teaches the supreme authority of the Scriptures, the sovereignty of God, predestination, and the doctrines of grace. These doctrines were the response of the Synod of Dort (1618–1619) to the Arminians' remonstrance (protest). Arminians are followers of Jacobus Arminius (1560–1609), a Dutch theologian, born in Oudewater, the Netherlands, who rejected the Reformers' understanding of predestination. Arminians typically teach that God's predestination of individuals was based on His foreknowledge of their accepting or rejecting Christ by their own free will.

created the world *ex nihilo*—out of nothing. But He re-creates a man out of a corrupt mass. It is parallel with the very resurrection of our Savior from the dead.

I understand that in preaching there are men with different gifts—teachers, preachers, and expositors, and all of them are very necessary for the health of the church. But you must understand this. I have heard of old G. Campbell Morgan,[6] that when he would go up that majestic tower in his church building to preach, he would quote to himself, "as a lamb to the slaughter, and as a sheep before his shearers" (Isa. 53:7). He knew that apart from a magnificent manifestation of the regenerating work of the Holy Spirit, everything he said would be death. It is the Spirit that gives life (John 6:63).

In that sense every one of us who proclaims the truth of God's Word must proclaim it as a prophet. What do I mean by that? I mean that we are always like Ezekiel standing in that valley of dry bones—and they are very dry (Ezek. 37:1–2)! We walk into that valley, and what do we do? We prophesy. We say, "Hear the word of the Lord." We know that the wind of God must blow on these slain ones, or they will not rise again. When you have fully grasped that—in the innermost part of your being— you will no longer give yourself to the manipulation that is often carried out in the name of evangelism. Instead, you will proclaim the Word of God.

---

6. G. Campbell Morgan (1863–1945) was a British evangelist preacher, and scholar. He was the pastor of Westminster Chapel in London before D. Martyn Lloyd-Jones.

Think of what such a preacher had to face. Consider dear George Whitefield. Everybody at that time believed they were Christian, thoroughly Christian. Why? Because they were baptized as infants, brought into the "covenant," and confirmed. But they lived like devils! Regeneration was traded for a type of mere creedalism that was given authority by the religious leaders of that day.[7]

Whitefield and the Wesleys told people, It is not right with your soul. You are not born again! There is no evidence of spiritual life. Examine yourself. Test yourself to see if you are in the faith (2 Cor. 13:5). Make your calling and election sure (2 Peter 1:10). "Ye must be born again" (John 3:7).

In America and elsewhere, because of the last several decades of modern evangelism, the true idea of being "born again" is totally lost. Now it means only that at one time in a crusade, you made a decision of some kind and you think you were sincere. But there is no evidence of a supernatural re-creating work of the Holy Spirit in your life. "If *any* man"—not if some men only—"be in Christ, he is a new creature" (2 Cor. 5:17, emphasis added).

We face the same battle now as in the time of the Wesleys and Whitefield. In America the issue is not infant baptism, nor "high church" confirmation by an ecclesiastical authority, though it may be in some parts of the world. What we often face now is the so-called sinner's

---

7. By creedalism I refer to outwardly following a formal creed or statement of faith without a new heart, without saving faith, and without a true heart love for God.

prayer. I want you to know, if I have declared war on anything, it is the sinner's prayer.

The sinner's prayer is the golden calf of today for the
Baptists, the evangelicals, and everyone else who has
followed them in this. The sinner's prayer has sent more
people to hell than nearly anything else on the face of
the earth!

You ask, "How can you say such a thing?" I answer,
"Take me to Scripture and show me, please, where anyone evangelized that way." The Scripture does not say
that Jesus Christ came to the nation of Israel and said,
"The time is fulfilled, and the kingdom of God is at hand.
Now who would like to ask Me into their hearts? I see
that hand." That is not what it says! Christ said, "Repent
ye, and believe the gospel" (Mark 1:15)!

Men today are trusting in the fact that at least one time
in their life they prayed a prayer, and someone told them
they were saved because they were sincere enough. And
so if you ask them "Are you saved?" they do not say, "Yes
I am, because I am looking unto Jesus and there is mighty
evidence giving me assurance of being born again." No!
They say instead, "One time in my life I prayed a prayer."
Now they live ungodly lives, but they prayed a prayer! I
heard of one evangelist who was coaxing a man to do that
thing. Finally, the man felt so uncomfortable, the evangelist
said, "Well, I'll tell you what. I will pray to God for you and
if it is what you want to say to God, squeeze my hand."

Is that the power of God? This is decisionism—the
idolatry of mere decisionism! Men think they are going to
heaven because they have judged the sincerity of their own
decision. When Paul came to the church in Corinth, he did

not say to them, "Look, you are not living like Christians, so let's go back to that one moment in your life when you prayed that prayer, and let's see if you were sincere." No, he said to them, "Examine yourselves, whether ye be in the faith; prove your own selves" (2 Cor. 13:5).

I want you to know, my friends, that salvation is by faith alone! It is a work of God. It is a grace upon grace upon grace. But the evidence of conversion is not just your examination of your sincerity at the moment of your conversion. It is the ongoing fruit in your life.

Look at what we have done! Is a tree not known by its fruit (Matt. 7:20)? Today 60 or 70 percent of Americans think they are converted, born again. But we kill thousands of babies a day! And we are hated around the world for our immorality. Yet we think we are Christian. And I lay the blame for this squarely at the feet of the preachers.

5

An Unbiblical Gospel Invitation

The time is fulfilled, and the kingdom of God is at hand: repent ye, and believe the gospel.

—Mark 1:15

I have seen the problem of an unbiblical gospel invitation everywhere. Whether they call themselves Calvinist or Arminian, so many preachers have in common the same superficial invitation. They talk a lot about many things and then they come to the invitation, and it is almost as though everyone loses their minds.

So walk up to someone and say, "God loves you and has a wonderful plan for your life." Can you imagine telling that to an American? "Sir, God loves you and has a wonderful plan for your life."

"What? God loves me? Well," says that person, "that's great because I love me too. Oh, this is wonderful. And God's got a wonderful plan? I've got a wonderful plan for my life too. And if I accept Him into my life, I'll have my best life now. This is absolutely wonderful."

That is not biblical evangelism. Let me give you something in its place. God comes to Moses, and He says,

> The LORD, the LORD God, merciful and gracious, long-suffering, and abundant in goodness and truth, keeping mercy for thousands, forgiving iniquity and transgression and sin, and that will by no means clear the guilty; visiting the iniquity of the fathers upon the children, and upon the children's children, unto the third and to the fourth generation. (Ex. 34:6–7)

What was the reaction of Moses? "Moses made haste, and bowed his head toward the earth, and worshipped" (Ex. 34:8).

Evangelism begins with the nature of God. Who is God? Can a man recognize anything about his sin if he has no standard with which to compare himself? If we tell that man nothing but trivial things about God that merely tickle the carnal mind,[1] will he ever be brought to genuine repentance and faith?

So we do not and cannot begin with, "God loves you and has a wonderful plan." We must begin with a discourse of the full counsel of who God is. And we must tell the person from the start it may cost him his life (Matt. 16:24)!

And then, after that beginning, many have these shallow exploratory questions: "Hey, you know you are a sinner, don't you?" That would be like, years ago, when my mother was dying of cancer, the doctor walking in and saying cheerfully, "Hey, Barb, you know you've got cancer, don't you?" We treat it so superficially. There is no weight, no solemnity. Instead, we must tell them, "Sir,

---

1. That is, the mind of the carnal or unconverted man, as opposed to a spiritual or Christian man.

there is a terrible malady upon you and a judgment coming." Because if you just tell a man, "Sir, did you know that you are a sinner?" you do not touch heart conviction at all. Go ask the devil if he knows he is a sinner. He will say, "Well, yes, I am. A mighty good one at that, or a mighty bad one depending on how you look at it. But, yes—I know I am a sinner."

The question, then, is not "Do you know that you are a sinner?" The question, in effect, must be this: "Is the Holy Spirit so at work in your heart, through the preaching of the gospel, that a change has been wrought, so that the sin you once loved you now hate, and the sin you once desired to embrace, you are wanting to run from it as though you were running from a dragon?"

After those shallow questions, people today might then ask, "Do you want to go to heaven?" This is the reason I would not let my children go to the vast majority of the Sunday schools and vacation Bible schools in evangelical churches. Some well-meaning person stands up and says, "Isn't Jesus wonderful?" after showing the Jesus film.

"Yes," the children respond.

"How many of you little children love Jesus?"

"Oh, I do."

"Who wants to accept Jesus into their little heart?"

"Oh, I do."

And then they get baptized! And they may walk like Christians for a little while because they have been taught well. They are being raised in a Christian culture, or at least a church culture. But when they turn fifteen or sixteen, when they have a developing show of their strength of will, they begin to break the bonds. They begin to live in wickedness. And then we go after them saying, "You are Christians, but you are just not living like it. Stop your backsliding."

Instead, we should go to them more biblically and say, "You made a confession of faith in Christ. You professed Him even in baptism, but now it seems as though you have turned away from Him. Examine yourself. Test yourself. There is little evidence of any true conversion in you!"

Then after college, when they are twenty-four or twenty-five, or maybe thirty, they come back to church and "rededicate their life." They join right in with that pseudo-Christian morality that encompasses "churchianity" in America. And in the last great day, they will hear this: "I never knew you: depart from me, ye that work iniquity" (Matt. 7:23).

You might say, "You are so angry, so cruel, so dismissive." Have I not a right to be righteously angry? Is it cruel to speak the truth in love? Is it dismissive to expose a false hope? Somebody must be crying out for revival. But we have not even got the foundations straight. Oh, that revival would come and straighten our foundations! While we have open eyes and ears, and have Scripture in front of us, should we not correct these things about the gospel invitation?

Why, then, do we ask, "Would you like to go to heaven?" My dear friend, everybody in their right mind wants to go to some kind of heaven, but they do not want God to be there when they get there! The question is not, then, "Do you want to go to heaven?" The question must be this: "Do you want God? Have you stopped being a hater of God? Has Christ become precious to you? Do you desire Him?"

That is what political theory is all about. Everybody wants to go to heaven, but men are haters of God. So the question is not, "Do you want to go to a special place where you will no longer hurt and you will get everything you want?" The question is "Do you want God? Has Christ become precious to you?"

Often, to get a person to pray the sinner's prayer, he is asked, "Would you like to go to heaven?"

"Well, yes," is the reply.

"Well, then, would you like to pray and ask Jesus into your heart?"

Please understand me clearly. There *are* people who get saved using that methodology, but it is not because of it. It is in spite of it.

Instead, we must ask people, "Sir, do you desire Christ? Do you see your sin?"

"Oh, yes, yes, I do."

"Sir, let's look at a few Scriptures here that lay out for us what repentance looks like. Is the Spirit bearing witness that these things are happening in your life? Do you see brokenness? Do you see the disintegration of everything you thought, and now your mind is filled with new thoughts about God and new desires and new hope?"

"Yes, I see that."

"Sir, that may be the firstfruits of repentance. Now, throw yourself upon Christ. Trust in Him. Trust in Him!"

Preacher, you have the authority to tell men the gospel. You have authority to tell men how to be saved, and you have authority to teach men biblical principles of assurance. But you have no authority to tell men they are saved. That is the work of the Holy Spirit of God!

But instead, many take them through that little ritual: "Did you ask Jesus into your heart?"

"Yes," he replies.

"Do you think you were sincere?"

"Yes."

"Do you think He saved you?"

"I don't know."

"Of course He saved you," the false preacher replies, "because you were sincere and He promised that if you asked Him to come in, He would come in. So you are saved."

And that man, or that woman, that child, walks out of the church after five minutes of counseling, and then the evangelist goes to lunch, and the person is still lost!

It is an unbiblical invitation and an unbiblical assurance. If that person ever doubts his or her salvation, then the preacher does the same thing all over again. He might say again, "Was there ever a point in time in your life when you prayed and asked Jesus to come in?"

"Yes."

"Were you sincere?"

"I think so."

"Then your present doubts are the devil bothering you."

And if that person lives without spiritual growth—even in the context of a church—in a life of continued carnality, there is still no doubt, no fear, no question. We simply blame it on the lack of personal discipleship, and we write it off as the doctrine of "the carnal Christian."

This idea of the carnal Christian has destroyed more lives and sent more people to hell than you can imagine! Do Christians struggle with sin? Yes. Can a Christian fall into sin? Absolutely. Can a Christian live in a continuous state of carnality all the days of his life, not bearing fruit, and truly be Christian? Absolutely *not*, or every promise in the Old Testament regarding the New Testament covenant of preservation has failed, and everything God said about discipline in Hebrews is a lie (Heb. 12:6)! A tree is known by its fruit (Luke 6:44).

I have seen preachers who understood much about the things of God. Then, when they have given an exemplary gospel presentation, they will enter, once again, into this unbiblical methodology.

Let me tell you a story about one of the most precious moments in my life as a Christian. I was preaching in Canada, just thirty kilometers from Alaska. There really were more grizzly bears in the town than there were people! It was a little church of about fifteen or twenty people. As I got up into the pulpit, a mountain of a man walked in, a man in his sixties or early seventies. And as I preached, as I saw his face, I threw everything else away and started preaching the gospel. He was the saddest human being I had ever seen. I simply preached the gospel, and when I was done, I walked from the pulpit directly to him.

I said, "Sir, what is wrong? What is troubling your soul?"

I have never seen a man so sad and downhearted in all my life. He pulled out a manila envelope. It contained some X-rays that I could not understand. But he said,

"I just came from the doctor. I am going to die in three weeks." That is what he told me. He said, "I have lived all my life on a working cattle ranch. You can get there only by float plane or riding horses across the mountains. I have never been to church. I have never read a Bible. I believe there is a God, and one time I heard somebody talking about some guy named Jesus. I have never been afraid of anything in my life—and I am terrified."

I said, "Sir, did you understand the message, the gospel?"

He said, "Yes."

Now what would a great majority of preachers have done at that moment? What might they have said? "Well, would you like to ask Jesus to come into your heart?"

I said, "Sir, you understood it?"

He said, "I understood it, but is that it? A child could have understood that. Is that all it is, that I understand it and I pray, or...?"

I said, "Sir, you are going to die in three weeks. I have to leave tomorrow. I will cancel my plane ticket and we will stay here over the Scriptures wrestling and crying out to God until you are either converted or you die and go to hell."

So we began. I began in the Old Testament, then the New Testament, every verse of Scripture dealing with the promises of God regarding redemption and salvation, over and over, time after time, reading John 3:16, praying for a while, crying out to God, questioning the man regarding repentance, regarding faith, regarding assurance—working until Christ had been formed in him.

And then finally, that evening, we were simply exhausted. There was no breakthrough; there was nothing. And I said, "Sir, let's pray." And we prayed.

Then I said, "Sir, read John 3:16 again."

He said, "We have read this a million times."

I said, "I know, but it is one of the greatest promises of salvation. Read that text again."

And I will never forget it. He had my Bible on his lap in those big mountainous hands of his and he said, "OK." And as he read, "For God so loved the world, that He gave..." he paused. Then he murmured, "I'm saved." He cried out, "I'm saved! Brother Paul, all my sins are gone! I have eternal life! I'm saved!"

I asked, "How do you know?"

He replied, "Haven't you ever read this verse before?"

What was going on? A working of the Spirit of God instead of those little tricks men try. What! You finish preaching and you only want to go and eat? No, after the preaching is when the work begins! Then comes dealing with souls. People may come forward in meetings for counsel by someone who should not be counseling. And after five minutes they are given the sinner's prayer to pray and a card to sign. And then—quick—give the card to the pastor, and the pastor says, "I would like to present to you a new child of God. Welcome him into the family of God." How dare any man play with salvation like this!

If you are going to present him, you might say this: "This man tonight has made a profession of faith in Jesus Christ. Because of our fear of God and our love for the souls of men, we will now be working with him to make sure that Christ has truly been formed in him, that he truly has a biblical understanding of repentance and faith, and great assurance and joy in the Holy Spirit. That is what we are going to do."

Look at what we have done in modern Christianity. I plead with you, look at what we are doing. And this is not some strange cult—this is us! I am talking about what is normal in modern evangelicalism. I plead with you: stop it. Please, stop it!

6

An Ignorance Regarding the Nature of the Church

That thou mayest know how thou oughtest to behave thyself in the house of God, which is the church of the living God, the pillar and ground of the truth.
—1 Timothy 3:15

God has only one religious institution—the church. Our ultimate goal and the ultimate product of revival in this world will be the planting of biblical churches. I have the greatest fear that the local church today is despised. Tell somebody that you are an itinerant preacher, that you have a worldwide ministry, and they all bow down. Tell someone you are a pastor of a group of thirty, and they make you feel as though you are a failure. Jesus Christ is not the prince of itinerant preachers; He is the prince of pastors.

Several years ago, Bill Clinton had a slogan during the presidential election campaign: "It's the economy, stupid!" My pastor at that time—one of the elders in our church, the primary teaching and preaching pastor—said to me one day, "You know, I'd like to have a bunch of shirts made up."

"What would they say?" I asked.

"It's the church, stupid!"

Jesus gave His life for His church, a beautiful, virgin, pristine church. If you want to give your life for something in the ministry, give it to the church—to a specific church, a body of believers, a local congregation. It is all about the church.

Understand this: there is not a remnant of believers in the church. You probably know about the remnant theology. This is the teaching that throughout all the course of Israel's history, national Israel was the people of God in one sense but that within the nation there existed a remnant of true believers. That is not true about the church. There is not a remnant of believers or a small group of believers inside a larger group called the church. True believers in the church are the remnant.

If pastors have ever come close to blaspheming, it is with regard to this. I hear theologians, itinerant teachers, and pastors saying these sorts of things: "There is just as much sin in the church as out of the church. There is just as much divorce in the church as out of the church. There is just as much immorality and pornography in the church as out of the church." And then preachers say, "Yes, the church is acting like a whore." You ought to be very careful calling the bride of Jesus Christ a whore.

I will tell you what the problem is: that pastors and preachers do not actually know what the church is. I want you to know that the church of Jesus Christ in America is beautiful. She is frail at times. She is weak. She is buffeted. She is not perfect. But I want you to know that she is brokenhearted, humbly walking with her God. The problem is that we do not really know what the church is.

Today, because of the lack of biblical preaching, the so-called church is filled with carnal, wicked people identified with Christianity. And then, because of all the goats in the midst of the lambs, the lambs are blamed for all the things the goats are doing. And then the name of God is blasphemed among the gentiles because of us (Rom. 2:24).

We should read what the Lord says through his servant Jeremiah:

> Behold, the days come, saith the LORD, that I will make a new covenant with the house of Israel, and with the house of Judah: Not according to the covenant that I made with their fathers in the day that I took them by the hand to bring them out of the land of Egypt; which my covenant they brake, although I was an husband unto them, saith the LORD: But this shall be the covenant that I will make with the house of Israel; After those days, saith the LORD, I will put my law in their inward parts, and write it in their hearts; and will be their God, and they shall be my people. And they shall teach no more every man his neighbour, and every man his brother, saying, Know the LORD: for they shall all know me, from the least of them unto the greatest of them, saith the LORD: for I will forgive their iniquity, and I will remember their sin no more. (Jer. 31:31–34)

Now I do not want to take away anything from the people called Israel, but this text is also applied to the church. I do not want to get into any battles on eschatology, but in the Bible, in the New Testament, this passage is applied to the people of God.

In Jeremiah 31:32, God says, "Not according to the covenant that I made with their fathers in the day that I took them by the hand to bring them out of the land of

Egypt." I hear preachers saying all the time, "When you look back and you see Israel, you see a bunch of godless people, idolaters. And in the midst of them there was a tiny remnant of true believers." That is true, but don't apply that to the New Testament church, because God says, I am going to do something different, something that is not like the covenant that I made with their fathers in the day I took them by the hand to bring them out of the land of Egypt—My covenant that they broke, although I was a husband to them. But this is the covenant I will make with the house of Israel after those days: I will put My law within them.

If you are converted, God has not given you a stone tablet of laws. He has supernaturally, through the reality of regeneration, written those laws in your heart. And because He has done that, He says, "I...will be their God, and they shall be my people" (v. 33).

And look what it says: "And they shall teach no more every man his neighbour, and every man his brother, saying, Know the LORD: for they shall all know me, from the least of them unto the greatest of them, saith the LORD: for I will forgive their iniquity, and I will remember their sin no more" (v. 34).

Again, this is the doctrine, the reality, of regeneration. God has been doing a new work these last two thousand years. We do not have a lot of churches in America. We have a lot of really nice brick buildings and finely manicured lawns! Just because someone says that they are of the church or they are Christian does not make it so. Look at what God says: they will not have to teach one another. That does not mean that there will not be teachers and preachers, but there will be an outstanding knowledge of God among them all, particularly with regard to their sins having been forgiven.

Look further at Jeremiah 32:38–40:

> And they shall be my people, and I will be their God: And I will give them one heart, and one way, that they may fear me for ever, for the good of them, and of their children after them: And I will make an everlasting covenant with them, that I will not turn away from them, to do them good; but I will put my fear in their hearts, that they shall not depart from me.

"And they shall be my people, and I will be their God." God does not say, "I hope so...maybe...if I get lucky...if I can get enough evangelists to work with Me... maybe this will all come out right." He says, in essence, "I am going to bring to Myself a people for Me, a people that I am going to give to my Son." The Lord says, "They shall be my people, and I will be their God."

Then he says, "And I will give them one heart, and one way." Do you see the contrast? The 1970s and the 1980s had many "Jesus marches," and thousands of people weeping and crying such things as, "The church is so divided. The church is not one." But if the church is not one, this new covenant promise is undermined, even violently assaulted. There would be a prayer that God the Father had not answered for His Son:

> Holy Father, keep through thine own name those whom thou hast given me, that they may be one, as we are.... Neither pray I for these alone, but for them also which shall believe on me through their word; That they all may be one; as thou, Father, art in me, and I in thee,

> that they also may be one in us: that the world may
> believe that thou hast sent me. And the glory which
> thou gavest me I have given them; that they may be
> one, even as we are one. (John 17:11, 20–22)

I submit to you that the true church is one! She has always been one. Have you ever sat down on an airplane, or maybe in a marketplace, and met someone you did not even know? And you, being truly evangelical, truly Christian, talk to him for no more than a few minutes, and you discover that he is a believer. This is a live one! This is the real thing. And, at that moment, you know you would give your life for him if need be.

Once we were in the mountains of Peru during the time of the civil war. We rode for twenty-two hours in the back of a grain truck under a black tarpaulin. At about midnight the truck stopped. We pulled off the cover and jumped into the jungle. We stayed that night just at the edge of the jungle and made our way up to a small town on the mountain. About halfway up my friend, Paco, and I got lost in the dark. We were praying, "Oh, God, give us some direction. We are lost. If we are found here, the terrorists own this place. The military would not even come in to find us." We cried out, "Oh, God, give us some direction. Help us!"

We heard a bell. And then we heard somebody talking. It was a strange conversation at first, we thought. Then we realized it was a little boy coming in from the fields talking with his burro, his donkey. And so we got behind him and followed him. Then we came to the edge of a little village, with huts and adobe homes. I said, "Paco, you know, if terrorists own this thing, we are dead."

"Yes," he replied, "but we have come to somewhere." So we came out, walked up to a man in the dark who was drunk, and said, "Are there brothers here?" because everybody knows what that means in the mountains—a "brother" is a real Christian.

The drunk man told us, "The old woman over there." So I went to this old Nazarene woman, and I knocked on the door. I said, "I am an evangelical pastor. Please help us!"

That old woman reached out with her lantern, grabbed me, and pulled me inside. She grabbed Paco. Her house was cut out of a cliff in the mud, and she took us down into a basement where there were some hay and chickens. She sat us down there and lit a lamp. Then a little boy came in, and she called to him, "Go and get the other brothers." Men started coming in from nowhere, bringing chickens and yucca and everything else, risking their lives for us! Why? Because the church of Christ is one!

We need to stop saying all these silly things—that the body of Christ is divided, that it is a mess and full of sin. I would not talk about the bride of Christ that way if I were you.

What you actually have in so many congregations today is a bunch of goats among the sheep, the sowing of tares among the wheat (Matt. 25:31–46; 13:24–30). Because very little biblical, compassionate church discipline is practiced, goats live among the sheep and wolves feed on and destroy the sheep. And those of you who are leaders in such churches are going to pay a high penalty when you stand before the One who loves them, because you did not have enough courage to stand up and confront the wicked.

The average scenario in North America with regard to churches, by and large, is that the churches are democracies. I do not want to get into the pros and cons of that. But because the preaching of the gospel is so low, the majority of the church consists of carnal lost people. Then, because the church is run as a democracy, the unconverted people, by and large, govern the direction of the church. Because the pastor does not want to lose the greatest number of the people, and because he has wrong ideas regarding evangelism and true conversion, he caters to the wicked in his church. So his little group of true sheep, who truly belong to Jesus Christ, are sitting there in the midst of all the theater, worldliness, and multimedia. They are crying out, "We just want to worship Jesus. We just want someone to teach us the Bible!" Dear friends, these pastors are going to pay for the terrible condition of their churches.

Many pastors are trying to keep together a bunch of wicked people, while a little flock in their midst is starving to death and made to go in directions they do not want to go. They are made to go along with the carnal majority!

Suppose my wife were at a store late one night and, as a man, you walked by and saw several men abusing her, and you put your head down in the name of self-preservation and simply walked by. I would not only look for those men—I would also come looking for you! The church is the bride of Christ, and she is precious to Him. He is concerned for her and for how you and I look at her and deal with her. It is going to cost you to serve the Jesus who loves His church. It could cost you your church, your reputation, and your denomination—it could cost you absolutely everything. But the bride of Jesus Christ is worth it!

Look at what God says: "I will give them one heart, and one way." And what is that way? It is Christ and His holiness. All true believers I have ever met speak much of Christ. They have a desire to be more holy than they are, more conformed to Christ.

The Lord speaks plainly: "I will give them one heart, and one way, that they may fear me for ever, for the good of them, and of their children after them: and I will make an everlasting covenant with them, that I will not turn away from them, to do them good." So many lost, wicked people, who nevertheless go to church on Sunday, hear this verse. They say to themselves, "Yes, God has made an everlasting covenant with me. He will never turn away from me—never, never. I am secure because of God's grace." But those lost men and women fail to read the second part.

There God says, "I will make an everlasting covenant with them, that I will not turn away from them, to do them good; but I will put my fear in their hearts, that they shall not depart from me." The evidence that God has made an everlasting covenant with you is that He has put the fear of God in you, so that you will not turn away from Him. If you turn away from Him and He does not discipline you, and you continue turning away from Him, it is evidence that He has not put His fear in you. This is evidence that you have not been regenerated— you actually have no covenant with God at all! This, dear friends, is biblical truth.

7

A Lack of Loving Church Discipline

Brethren, if a man be overtaken in a fault, ye which are spiritual, restore such an one in the spirit of meekness; considering thyself, lest thou also be tempted.

—Galatians 6:1

Matthew 18:15–17 says this:

> Moreover if thy brother shall trespass against thee, go and tell him his fault between thee and him alone: if he shall hear thee, thou hast gained thy brother. But if he will not hear thee, then take with thee one or two more, that in the mouth of two or three witnesses every word may be established. And if he shall neglect to hear them, tell it unto the church: but if he neglect to hear the church, let him be unto thee as an heathen man and a publican.

Most evangelical pastors in America today ought to take that passage and rip it right out of their Bible, so much do they neglect it. Of course, you cannot do that. You must take the whole Bible or not any of it at all! Many pastors leave their theology behind when they come out of their study. They are theological in conversation and in their office. But when they step out of their office, they run the church by carnal means.

I am not an elder at my church, so I can say the following without boasting: our church practices church discipline. I have been a member of a very large church, with about one thousand attending. The pastors there estimated that they saved thirty marriages over several years through loving, compassionate church discipline—discipline that does not begin with excommunication. It begins with "Ye which are spiritual, restore."

Some might say, "We can't practice discipline—we are just too loving." Are you more loving than Jesus? He is the One who commanded this!

"Oh," you say, "but, it will cause so many problems." You are absolutely right! Maybe that is why there is not much difference between the church and worldly culture today—we are not confronting the culture around us. And we do not confront culture by going out there and picketing Hollywood. We confront culture by obeying God! Noah built the ark and condemned the world. You do not need to have a protest sign. Just walk in obedience, and the world will hate you.

"If thy brother shall trespass against thee, go and tell him his fault between thee and him alone: if he shall hear thee, thou hast gained thy brother" (Matt. 18:15). What a wonderful thing! "But if he will not hear thee, then take with thee one or two more, that in the mouth of two or three witnesses every word may be established" (Matt. 18:16). Friends, the witnesses are not there to be on your side. No, they are there to listen objectively and to render a judgment. Maybe you are the one who is wrong. Maybe your brother is not in sin; maybe you are overcritical and legalistic.

"If he shall neglect to hear them, tell it unto the church: but if he neglect to hear the church, let him be unto thee as an heathen man and a publican." In other words, treat that person as an outsider and a tax collector. We need to hear and to heed this. Either we start obeying God and disciplining ourselves or we can have God discipline us. Maybe the hour is come when that is going to happen!

I am not talking about critical, legalistic, hateful men—there are enough of those. I am talking about a pastor, a group of elders—leaders who love enough to lay their lives on the line because they know that this is not a game. This is not something that we do just for this life; eternity is at stake—the salvation of souls. Look at the old books from men like Spurgeon and Whitefield, works from the Puritans and the Reformers. Many of those books dealt with the gospel—what it is, how to preach it, how to bring someone to Christ, how to discern true conversion, how to become a physician of souls.

In such matters, many churches have joined Rome. In the Roman Catholic Church, the baby is baptized and is pronounced "Christian." Henceforth, the baby belongs to Rome. Never again do you deal with conversion. You just create all sorts of worldly means to try to keep them in the church! And many evangelical preachers have done the same thing. Pray a little prayer with people after two or three minutes of counseling, after half an hour of preaching, twenty-five minutes of which was nothing but humorous stories. Then you draw the net for five minutes at the end. Talk to them for a little bit and declare them saved. Then you spend the rest of your days trying to disciple them, wondering why they do not grow!

I believe in personal one-on-one discipleship. But understand that the church largely got along without it for more than a thousand years, without what we now know as personal discipleship and all the books and helps available today. I want you to think about this. One-on-one discipleship became gigantic in the late seventies and remains so today. What is the cry? "Just as many people are going out the back doors," they say, "as are coming in the front doors, and the reason why this is happening is because we are not discipling people." No! The reason why it is happening is because people are not getting converted. They show themselves as unconverted because Christ's sheep hear His voice and follow Him (John 10:3), whether you disciple them or not.

Now we ought to disciple people, but that is not why they are leaving. "They went out, that they might be made manifest that they were not all of us" (1 John 2:19). And they hardly got a chance to be "of us" because they never heard a true gospel—no one ever dealt with their souls. So we spend a fortune discipling goats, hoping they will become sheep. You cannot teach a goat to become a sheep. A goat becomes a sheep only by the supernatural working of the Spirit of almighty God.

I commit myself and my family to a faithful church because it practices church discipline and because I need to be under church discipline. I need the watchful care of elders and other members who take this seriously. If my children make a profession of faith and then go awry, I want to know that they will be brought before the church, if necessary, for the salvation of their souls.

Some of you would get so angry if a pastor walked up to you and said, "Honestly, I have been praying about your child and I fear that he is unconverted." You would get so mad, you would rally a group to have that pastor kicked out. Perhaps you should instead be saying, "Praise God, we have got a man of God here."

V

8

A Silence on Separation

Be ye not unequally yoked together with unbelievers: for what fellowship hath righteousness with unrighteousness?

—2 Corinthians 6:14

Today there is a void of serious teaching about holiness in life. There is, of course, a general teaching on holiness that everyone agrees on. "Let us be holy," they say, "we need to be more holy. Why not have a holiness conference?" But when you get specific about what that means, everything boils over.

"Follow peace with all men," the writer of Hebrews tells us, "and holiness, without which no man shall see the Lord" (Heb. 12:14). Does anybody believe this? A pastor says, "But I have been blamed so often for teaching 'works' religion." This goes back again to the principle of regeneration and the providence of God. If God truly converts a man, He will continue working in that man, through teaching, blessing, admonition, and discipline. He will see to it that the work He has begun will be finished. And that is why the writer says that without holiness, "no man shall see the Lord." Why? Because if there is no growth in holiness, then God is not working in your life. And if He is not working in your life, it is because you are not His child!

Look at the difference between Jacob and Esau. "Jacob have I loved...Esau have I hated" (Rom. 9:13). Yet God fulfilled all His promises to both of them. Jacob was blessed; Esau was blessed. How did God demonstrate His judgments and wrath against Esau and His love toward Jacob? First, He let them both run wild. But in Esau there was no work of discipline, no work of godly correction—nothing. This was the wrath of God on him! But God severely disciplined Jacob almost every day of his life. This was the love of God for him! It was the loving discipline, the correction of God, to bring him to holiness. And it is the same for all true believers today.

Furthermore, the Lord says through Paul,

> I beseech you therefore, brethren, by the mercies of God, that ye present your bodies a living sacrifice, holy, acceptable unto God, which is your reasonable service. And be not conformed to this world: but be ye transformed by the renewing of your mind, that ye may prove what is that good, and acceptable, and perfect, will of God. (Rom. 12:1–2)

Why does he say to "present your bodies"? I think the reason is to avoid all this "super-spirituality" of today. You say, "I have given Jesus my heart, and you can't judge a book by its cover. You can't judge my inner condition by my outer works." But, as a matter of fact, you *can* judge a book by its cover. Jesus never said you could not judge a man's inner condition by his outward works. He specifically said that you could: "The tree is known by his fruit" (Matt. 12:33).

If you think that you have given Christ your heart, then He will have your body too. And I will tell you why. The heart, my friend, is not some blood-pumping muscle or some figment of a poet's imagination. In the Bible, the language of "the heart" refers to the very essence or core of your being. Do not tell me that Jesus has the very essence and core of your being and that it does not affect your whole body and life. It just does not happen that way!

We need to go through Scripture not legalistically and not just drawing inferences but rather by standing on its clear commands. Commands about what? What sort of commands guide us?

I do not agree with everything the Puritans said, but I do love the Puritans. One of the reasons why I love them is because I believe they honestly made an attempt to bring everything in their lives under the lordship of Jesus Christ. Everything, such as their minds! They wrote eight-hundred-page books on what we should think about according to the Scriptures and what should not enter our minds according to the Scriptures. They wrote about what we should do with our eyes. They wrote about what should go in our ears and what should not go in our ears. They taught about how the tongue should be ruled. They talked about the whole direction of our lives and its details.

It might scare you, but the Bible also talks about how we should dress. I am going to be careful here, and I do not want to speculate. My wife says it this way: "If your clothing is a frame for your face from which the glory of

Christ springs forth, it is of God. But if your clothing is a frame for your body, it is sensual, and God hates it." The nature of God guides our decisions in every detail of our conduct.

The aim of this little book is not to address everything to do with our holiness. We know that holiness is not just outward expression. Nevertheless, we have come to be people who use the interior work of the Spirit as an excuse to say that nothing needs ever to happen on the outside. That is simply not true! Some of you may cry out that the Spirit of God would fill you and work in you, but it takes only a half hour of television to so grieve Him that He will be miles from you. If water is 99 percent pure, and 1 percent sewage, then I am not drinking it!

At one time I was struggling, and a friend of mine reported it in a conversation with Leonard Ravenhill. When he heard about the situation from my friend, he sent a tract to me. I still have that tract. I will never, never part with it. It said, "Others can; you cannot." I may not agree with everything in that tract, but I do know this: there are places I do not go, there are situations into which I do not put myself, not because I am holier than other people but because I know what I am!

You may know the story of one of the greatest violinists in Europe playing his final concert as an old man. When he finished, a young man, also a violinist, walked up to him, and said, "Sir, I'd give my life to play like you." And the old man said, "Son, I have given my life to play like me."

You say, "I want the power of God on my life." Do you? Then something has to go. "I want to know Him," you say. Then some separation from the world has to occur! Everyone else is running around in all their little retreats, getting together with group hugs, and singing "Kumbaya"[1] or whatever it may be. Perhaps you need to get alone in the wilderness with God, fasting for seven days on your knees and studying the book of Psalms. You need to be alone with God, belonging to Him. To be a man of God there must be times when even your wife—who is of your own flesh, one with you—looks you in the eye and knows that she cannot go with you into that hidden place with God into which you go.

Today in our churches there is a silence on separation from the world. The Scriptures are not silent. They demand from us an answer. "Be ye not unequally yoked together with unbelievers: for what fellowship hath righteousness with unrighteousness?" (2 Cor. 6:14). None! What fellowship has light with darkness (v. 14)? None! Darkness is the opposite of God's revelation. What harmony does Christ have with devils (v. 15)? None! What has the believer in common with the unbeliever (v. 15)? Nothing!

The Lord says, "Come out from among them" (v. 17). Come out from the midst of what? Come out from the midst of lawlessness, darkness, satanic devices, and the life and worldliness of the unbeliever. Come out from it!

---

1. An African spiritual song from the 1930s, popular in folk music, then later in youth camp gatherings, used here to represent superficial religion and emotionalism.

9

A Replacement of the Scriptures regarding the Family

Beware lest any man spoil you through philosophy and vain deceit, after the tradition of men, after the rudiments of the world, and not after Christ.

—Colossians 2:8

This ninth concern is very important to me as an older man with a young family. I didn't get married until I was thirty. My wife had a small brain tumor for the first eight years of our marriage. We could not have children, and then, praise God, He was pleased to grant us several.

Think about this. Our Sunday morning services are so cosmetic. Just because there seems to be beautiful worship, the sermon went well, and people seem to be moved is not evidence of real spirituality. I will tell you what the evidence is: the home, the marriages, the families. The Bible records the days in which "there was no king in Israel, but every man did that which was right in his own eyes" (Judg. 17:6). When I travel, and I meet all kinds of people, I try to find a godly man who has raised godly children, and I go and latch on to him. But in most cases do you know what I find out? Most of the people I talk to in church want to discuss old wives' tales and sociology and every other thing. It is all about what is right in their own eyes, and they cannot give me one Bible verse in defense of their view. But every once in a while I find a man and a woman who set themselves to rear their family according to Scripture. The difference is overwhelming!

When I am on an airplane, people will sit down beside me and ask, "What do you do?"

I reply, "Oh, I'm a husband."

They ask, "What else do you do?"

"Oh, I'm a father."

"What else do you do?"

"Well, if I have any time left over, I preach a little."

What does it matter if a man wins the whole world and loses his own family? Let me put it to you this way: On what basis are you rearing your children and loving your wife? On what is your family grounded? If you cannot start going into the Scriptures and showing me how your family is founded on it, I can almost assure you that you are a captive to psychology, sociology, and the whims and lies of this age. You see, you do not have the right to follow all these other things. You have no authority apart from the Word of God.

Look at Genesis 18:19. God says of Abraham, "For I know him, that he will command his children and his household after him, and they shall keep the way of the LORD, to do justice and judgment; that the LORD may bring upon Abraham that which he hath spoken of him." What a beautiful way this is!

Or consider what Paul says: "I beseech you therefore, brethren, by the mercies of God, that ye present your bodies a living sacrifice, holy, acceptable unto God, which is your reasonable service. And be not conformed to this world: but be ye transformed by the renewing of your mind, that ye may prove what is that good, and acceptable, and perfect, will of God" (Rom. 12:1–2). The second verse tells us that the will of God is perfect. If as a man of God you ever come up with the idea that "I am sacrificing my family for the sake of the ministry," I will tell you that you are lying. You are sacrificing your family for the sake of the little kingdom you are trying to build. I can say that because the will of God is perfect. That means I do not have to violate the will of God with regard to my family in order to fulfill the will of God with regard to my ministry. God does not need you! He does require, however, that you be obedient.

Someone once asked me whether I was against evangelism. I replied, "Yes and no. I am not against biblical evangelism, but I am against the way you are doing it." In the same way, someone might ask, "Are you against Sunday school and youth groups?" Again, my answer would be yes and no.

I want to give you two examples in order to explain what I mean. Perhaps for some this will not be strong enough, and for some I am going to be too strong. However, I want to use these two things to point out what is wrong with us.

With regard to Sunday school, no matter what denomination you are a part of, if it is some large denomination that is in any way organized, I can assure you that your denomination spends large amounts of dollars on Sunday school material, on teaching teachers how to teach

Sunday school, and on doing everything in the book to promote Sunday school.

So let me ask you, how much money does your denomination spend, and how many conferences and man-hours are invested, to teach fathers to teach their children? God doesn't have a plan B. He has only a plan A. When you circumvent plan A, you discover that plan B won't work!

Now I am not saying that children cannot come together in groups and be catechized or taught, but if that ever even begins to supplant the ministry of the father in the home, you must rectify this immediately!

Do you see what I am saying? Look at just this one small example: there is everything available for Sunday school. But there are few conferences in this country to teach men how to teach their children. And most of the time Sunday school is nothing more than entertainment, because Sunday school teachers do not have the authority to righteously discipline your child. And even if they did, most would not do it because they do not believe in it.

Now consider youth groups. "Well," says someone, "youth need to be together. They just need to be together." Really? What does Scripture say? "He that walketh with wise men shall be wise: but a companion of fools shall be destroyed" (Prov. 13:20). Young people need to be with adults so that they stop acting like naïve fools, join adulthood, and put away the foolishness that leads to their destruction. I am not saying you cannot bring youth together, but I submit that if you do, don't leave parents out of the picture!

And you say, "What about the lost young people who come into our church?" I ask, "What are they seeing now?" These lost youth come among your Christian young people in church and they see almost the same thing that they see in their own homes—no parents, and kids teaching kids. Or one guy a little bit older teaching other people's kids. But what would happen if a lost youth came into your church and saw the children and young people there in a loving, wonderful relationship with their parents? They would say, "Wow! I have never seen anything like this before. Look at this dad. He loves his son! And the son, he loves his dad! Look at the love. So is *this* Christianity?"

Our situation in the churches is very needy, but we tend to be blind to it. It is like the situation in which a man comes up to me with a bleeding forehead, and he says, "I have been everywhere. No one can diagnose my problem." And I say, "Well, I am no doctor, but I'll follow you around for twenty-four hours to see what we can see." And I notice that every time the hour strikes, he hits himself in the head with a brick. If it strikes one o'clock he hits himself one time. If it strikes two, he hits himself twice. If it strikes twelve, he hits himself twelve times in the head with the brick. After observing this, cautiously and carefully, taking notes for twenty-four hours, I come up to him and I say, "You know, I am no doctor, but I think I have figured out your problem."

It is that pathetic among us! Why do our children do what they do? Why is everything so turned upside down? It is like one dear saint who would not let his teenage son go out with a young lady to be in some private place.

Someone asked him one time, "Don't you trust your son?" He said, "No, I don't trust my son. Whatever made you think that? I don't even trust his dad! I wouldn't put his father alone with a woman who wasn't his wife, and yet I have much more to lose from impropriety than my son. And I have much more control of my will than a teenager with raging hormones. So what would make you ever think I would trust my son in that situation?"

We violate biblical principle after biblical principle, and then we wonder why everything is a mess.

10

Pastors Malnourished
in the Word of God

Study to shew thyself approved unto God, a workman that needeth not to be ashamed, rightly dividing the word of truth.

—2 Timothy 2:15

I was listening a few months ago to all the horrendous things that are happening to our country. (I don't know what you would call it anymore—a republic, a democracy, a socialistic state?). I was so burdened as I sat there listening. I was saying to myself, "Oh, God, what can I do? Right now, Lord, honestly, with all that is in me, I will jump in the middle of the fire. If there is a charging rhino, I will jump in front of it. Just tell me what to do! Do you want me to go to Washington and just stand in front of the White House and preach until they throw me in jail? I am tired of just preaching to Christians and in churches and conferences. Oh God, the country is going to hell! What do you want me to do? Just throw me at them."

Now consider 1 Timothy 4:1–16:

Now the Spirit speaketh expressly, that in the latter times some shall depart from the faith, giving heed to seducing spirits, and doctrines of devils; speaking lies in hypocrisy; having their conscience seared with a hot iron; forbidding to marry, and commanding to abstain from meats, which God hath created to be received with thanksgiving of them which believe and know the truth. For every creature of God is good, and nothing to be refused, if it be received with thanksgiving: for it is sanctified by the word of God and prayer.

If thou put the brethren in remembrance of these things, thou shalt be a good minister of Jesus Christ, nourished up in the words of faith and of good doctrine, whereunto thou hast attained. But refuse profane and old wives' fables, and exercise thyself rather unto godliness. For bodily exercise profiteth little: but godliness is profitable unto all things, having promise of the life that now is, and of that which is to come. This is a faithful saying and worthy of all acceptation. For therefore we both labour and suffer reproach, because we trust in the living God, who is the Saviour of all men, specially of those that believe. These things command and teach.

Let no man despise thy youth; but be thou an example of the believers, in word, in conversation, in charity, in spirit, in faith, in purity. Till I come, give attendance to reading, to exhortation, to doctrine. Neglect not the gift that is in thee, which was given thee by prophecy, with the laying on of the hands of the presbytery. Meditate upon these things; give thyself wholly to them; that thy profiting may appear to all. Take heed unto thyself, and unto the doctrine; continue in them: for in doing this thou shalt both save thyself, and them that hear thee.

The first verse says, "Now the Spirit speaketh expressly, that in the latter times some shall depart from the faith, giving heed to seducing spirits, and doctrines of devils." Paul goes on to tell young Timothy that, basically, all kinds of destruction are going to break loose in culture, that everything is just going to be maddening, with men acting as beasts! Conrad Mbewe[1] has said: "In Africa we no longer have a fear of beasts. We don't run from beasts. We fear men and run from men." He was, of course, talking about the effects of radical depravity in mankind. Paul tells us just that: "The world is going to come unglued, Timothy."

What else does he say? "If thou put the brethren in remembrance of these things, thou shalt be a good minister of Jesus Christ, nourished up in the words of faith" (v. 6). Yes, the world has lost its mind! God is telling us, "It is all under My providence, but listen to Me! Here should be your reaction in the midst of all sin breaking loose everywhere in the midst of apostasy, in the midst of persecution. Here is what you need to do: be constantly 'nourished up in the words of faith.'"

Instead, we always want to run out there and do something. We want to fix something. But God is seeking men of character, polished swords. First of all, be constantly "nourished up in the words of faith and of good doctrine, whereunto thou hast attained." This "whereunto thou hast attained" is very important. It means "that which you have been following." I think it is indicating to us that a simple intellectual study of Scripture will not achieve the goal that God has for His people. God's people must obey God's Word. They must begin following it.

---

1. Pastor of Kabwata Baptist Church, Lusaka, Zambia.

You cannot learn doctrine well until you follow the doctrine you learn!

And then Paul calls us to "refuse profane and old wives' fables" (v. 7). All this emergent church stuff, much of the church growth stuff, all the cultural sensitivity that throws biblical sensitivity out the window—it is just a bunch of little boys wanting to play church without the power of God in their life. It is David trying to fit himself into Saul's armor. To the wind with it! The more you trust in the arm of flesh, the less you are going to see the power of God.

Paul then says, "exercise thyself rather unto godliness" (v. 7); that is, discipline yourself for the purpose of godliness. Man of God, do you want revival? So do I. We need an army, though. If mighty, flaming pikes and swords and weaponry are to be dropped out of heaven for our fight, then we must be the caliber of men who can wield those things to fight with sound character. We should discipline ourselves for the purpose of godliness.

Discipline yourself to prayer. Discipline yourself to the systematic reading of Scripture from Genesis to Revelation over and over and over again. Discipline yourself in your speech. Discipline yourself in the company you keep. Discipline yourself in when you go to bed and when you rise up. This is a war. Discipline yourself!

If you are a younger man, under thirty, even under forty, being born in the age in which you have been born, unless you are some exception, you probably lack discipline because you have seldom been required to really work. You have never needed to work for your food. Your fathers probably never made you work so hard that your bones cried. The men who have accomplished much and have been used of God have been men of labor in the ministry. Effectual ministry is hard. It will cost you everything! And by the time you are an old man, you will be broken—but strong in the things of God!

"Exercise thyself rather unto godliness. For bodily exercise profiteth little: but godliness is profitable unto all things, having promise of the life that now is, and of that which is to come" (vv. 7–8). Who cares about "your best life now"? It is all about eternity! Someday you will stand in those granite halls before the Lord of glory, and kings and the greatest men on earth will be divided and split and culled. Some will be cast into eternal hell and some will be invited into eternal glory to live for eternity. These Olympic athletes, how majestic they are—but only for a moment. They start training when they are four and five years old. They never do anything but train until they are twenty-two. They run a nine-second race for a medal they hang up on a wall, and that is it! Their moment of glory is soon past, and all they have lived for is over! Can you not give equal effort for eternal things?

Some of the greatest men of God have been very limited in their bodies. In their abilities, they were so limited that they had to focus on one thing. They gave themselves to the ministry. "For bodily exercise profiteth little.... This is a faithful saying and worthy of all acceptation. For therefore we both labour and suffer reproach, because we trust in the living God" (vv. 8, 9–10). This is not some martyr thing in which we uselessly give our lives to nothing, only to be pulverized without hope. No! We serve God, and God will honor us. We fix our hope on Him, and He gives us strength!

This life is a vapor. When I first preached this message I was forty-seven years old, but I feel like yesterday I was twenty-one. Where did it all go? It is a vapor! While you have strength, preach! I praise God and His providence that, as a young man, I spent myself in the Andes Mountains and in the jungles of Peru, doing what I no longer have the strength to do.

While you are a young man, while there is strength in you, labor with all your might. Take those stupid video games of yours and crush them under your feet. Throw the TV out the window. You were made for greater things than these. If you are a child of the King, nothing on this earth can satisfy you—nothing! "These things command and teach" (v. 11).

Now, there is so much here, but look at verse 15: "Meditate upon these things; give thyself wholly to them; that thy profiting may appear to all." Let us say that my child spills a glass of water on a wooden table. By the laws that God has placed in nature, the water heaps up a bit on the table, so much that you can see it as a pool. You walk by it and you say, "There is water spilled on the table." It is apparent to all. But then I come by, take a towel, lay it across the pool of spilled water, and lift it up. And you say, "I no longer see any water." Where is it? It is absorbed into the towel. Men, you are to meditate on and absorb matters of biblical godliness and character. Pastors, I plead with you: you are not errand boys! You are not to spend your days catering to the whims of carnal churchmen. Get yourself in your study. Drink deep. Be so absorbed in the knowing of God that people say, "Where is he? He used to be such a man about town, such a friend to everyone, such a personable fellow. Where is he?" He is absorbed in these things!

We are men of God. We are ministers of the Most High. There should be an "otherness" about us. We should have a distant gaze in our eyes toward a distant star. The greatest thing we can do for our people is to be men of God, absorbed in the things of God, so that when we open our mouths the Word of God comes out.

The main preaching pastors in the churches to which I have belonged have always given themselves to study. In one church to which I belonged, I talked to the other leaders regarding the preaching pastor and said this: "Please do this one thing. Take as much of the burden off that brother as we possibly can and let him live in that study with God, because I have got children out here. And the greatest gift that man could give to me is to study to show himself approved, and to come out in that pulpit in the power of the Holy Spirit and proclaim, 'Thus saith the Lord,' correcting and rebuking, giving great promises and warnings. Please, do that for me."

Pastor, please do that for your people, because God says, "Take heed unto thyself, and unto the doctrine; continue in them: for in doing this thou shalt both save thyself, and them that hear thee" (1 Tim. 4:16). This verse means almost nothing in the evangelical community today. How many pastors and preachers do you think take it seriously? How many say to themselves, "I need to pay close attention to myself to ensure salvation for me and for those who hear me"?

I have a question for you, if you are a pastor. When was the last time you examined your own life to see if you were in the faith, to see if you really know the Lord? I have great assurance when I study my own conversion, when I discuss it with other men, when I look over the twenty-five years of my pilgrimage with Christ. I have great assurance of having come to know Him. But even now, if I were to depart from the faith, and walk away, and keep going in that direction—into heresy, into worldliness—it could be the greatest of proofs that I never knew Him, that the whole thing was a work of the flesh.

I know what I am saying is shocking to many. You may think, "Oh my, I have never heard such a thing," but this is the timeless biblical truth you need to hear. Just read *Pilgrim's Progress*.[2] "Take heed unto thyself, and unto the doctrine; continue in them: for in doing this thou shalt both save thyself, and them that hear thee."

May God bless His church!

---

2. The classic allegory by John Bunyan (1628–1688), in which the main character, Christian, seeks relief from the guilt-burden of the law, finds forgiveness at the cross of Christ, and proceeds to face many trials in this world on his way to eternal life in the Celestial City. At every turn, he finds he must rely on the Word of God to keep him on the straight and narrow path that God has marked out for him. On the way, he meets many false professors who seem at first to be pilgrims also, but most of them (Faithful and Hopeful excepted) fall away.